# A Wind From Nowhere

## Poems by Richard Schnap

To Fran

A Wind From Nowhere
Poems by Richard Schnap

Cover art & design: Richard Schnap

First Edition
Manufactured in the United States of America

ISBN-13: 978-1532803482

ISBN-10: 1532803486

All inquiries and permission requests should be addressed to Editor, Flutter Press, flutterpresseditor@outlook.com.

*Flutter Press*
*Flutterpress2009.blogspot.com*

# Acknowledgements

My deep gratitude goes to Sandy Benitez, who made this book a reality and in whose magazines *Poppy Road Review*, *Flutter Poetry Journal*, and *Black Poppy Review* these poems first appeared.

*For Alice*

Table of Contents

Portent
(In memory of Arthur A. Bell)

She stood looking down
At his grave as if
It was a door locked
With a buried key

Remembering how he said
That if he died
He would send her a sign
From the rumored beyond

And as a soft wind
Caressed her cheek
Like a loving hand
Wiping away her tears

A tiny white bird
Landed on his tombstone
And sang her a melody
She seemed to know by heart

Revelations in the Thrift Store

Here is a doll with a painted smile
And eyes as hollow as a ghost's
Here is a book by an obscure author
That's been out of print for a decade
Here is a dress from someone's closet
In fashion for only a season
Here is a chair that once faced a desk
From a company long out of business

And I see a young girl falling in love
Leaving her childhood behind her
And a pile of notebooks left by the curb
Their words disappearing in the rain
And a mirror in a chic department store
Reflecting what the stars now endorse
And an old man passing a vacant lot
Where once stood the story of his life

Hidden Faces

The sun rises through the crimson clouds
A ruby sewn into a red velvet gown

As I watch the morning news on TV
A horror film with a thousand sequels

Across the street the parking lot fills up
A barren shore buried by the tide

While crowded buses pass slowly by
Ships carrying immigrants to strange new lands

Then a siren wails off in the distance
A lonely witch casting a love spell

And a crowd of children are led to school
A cluster of roses yet to sprout thorns

As the bell tolls in the church on the corner
The heartbeat of a man kissing his wife

While I watch the white trail of a high flying plane
The ghost of a blackbird haunting the sky

Nocturne

He always felt better in the night
As if the shadow that haunted him by day
Faded in the arms of a greater darkness

It was then he became more alive
His senses sharpened so that he heard
Voices in the vast silence of another world

He listened to the soliloquy of the wind
An old man destined to sweep the earth
Like an immortal janitor who'd been born to it

The rain beating like a thousand drummers
An immense symphony in a timeless music
That was always the same and always different

But too soon the black curtain would rise
And the sun would climb up inch by inch
To bring a sad finale to his secret masterpiece

Until once again he could raise his eyes
To count the stars caught in the sky's web
The jewels in the sable hair of his beloved mistress

Genesis

The blank page stared at him
A naked white desert
A woman without a name

As he gripped his pen
A bird searching for water
A man waiting for a sign

Then the two began to touch
A river sprung from nowhere
A caress both sure and slow-moving

Till the void between them vanished
A garden of unknown flowers
Love in a strange new language

Eclipse

Some people want to save the world
Others want to run from it and hide

And some want both. I knew one once,
Who by day eased the suffering

Of hospital patients and by night
Medicated his own with Goth anthems

And anti-depressants. Then on weekends
He'd volunteer at an animal shelter

While buried in his drawer was the corpse
Of a pet tarantula. It was as if he was

His own dark twin, who stood before
His bathroom mirror every morning

Facing a double exposure staring
Back, one that was half saint

And half skeleton, alive yet dead,
In a world that had a place for each.

Bottle of the Soul

When I see an old man
Trudging past from the liquor store
With a beige plastic bag

I wonder if it holds
A black-labeled whiskey
Or a rose-colored wine

And if it's to mark
A fifty-year marriage
Or another night alone

In the arms of the dream
Either waiting at his window
Or in the shadows on his wall

Honorable Mention
(In memory of Melissa Schnap Marsh)

In her youth she studied acting
To audition for the role
Of the witch in "Sleeping Beauty"

Who then transformed into a beast
Breathing fire to consume
The frightened girl inside her soul

But she only landed parts
In second-rate romances
With the same low-budget script

The woman left abandoned
Within a haunted dollhouse
With the phantom of her dreams

Premonition

In his dream he heard
The fluttering of wings
By a starlit sea

As a tall lighthouse
With its guiding beacon
Was suddenly snuffed out

The very next day
An x-ray revealed
His brain held a tumor

And as he walked home
A murder of crows
Seemed to follow behind

Epilogue

He felt himself merging with the night,
Passing into shadow, weaving through the wall,

Above the houses, on invisible wings,
Robed in the wind, crowned with the stars,

As he looked down at the darkened city,
The world he'd known, the roads he'd traveled,

And thought: who was I really,
A stranger in a realm that others owned,

A visitor from a foreign land, only for a time,
Silently waiting in crowded rooms,

In long lines that never seemed to move,
But now released, riding a black train

Into a black tunnel, a white light ahead,
Becoming a face, its eyes like diamonds,

Its lips like a flower, till he faded into it,
Tasted its kiss, and dreamed no more.

Reincarnations

I have known cashiers
In supermarket checkout lines
Who used to be alchemists
Turning lead into gold

And I have known cab drivers
Working twelve-hour shifts
Who used to be soothsayers
Reading fortunes for a price

And I have known telemarketers
Soliciting for charities
Who used to be courtesans
In the harems of kings

And I have known dishwashers
Scraping plates in hot kitchens
Who used to be shaman
With the power to make it rain

Atlantis

I watch the cars glide slowly
Through the supermarket's parking lot
Fish weaving through the ruins
Of a buried civilization

While across the street the liquor store
Stands dark as an alcoholic's dream
A temple to an ancient deity
With the power to help one forget

For this is the drowned metropolis
The city abandoned beneath
Sunken in its own memories
Growing fainter every day

And someday archaeologists
May pick through its bricks and bones
To maybe discover lost diamonds
Or maybe just handfuls of dust

Portraits of the Heart

I didn't know their stories
Only hints from what spoke to them

In a gallery of collages
Where they each made one their own

A smiling man holding
A woman with a mirrored face

A hand in a room reaching
Past a ruined wall toward the sky

A desert highway curving
By a sign with a question mark

A woman on a road wandering
In the winter with her eyes closed

And when they left I wondered
Why they all seemed so alike

Like birds in an aviary
Caught in the same cage

# Shroud

Above the city's lights
Hang dull orange clouds

Stained with the shade
Of a century's rust

They make me remember
The long-gone mills

Whose bodies were razed
But whose spirits endure

I think of soldiers
Caught in the grip

Of a diabolical war
Whose wages were death

And even though their hands
Built the skeleton of a nation

Their souls find no rest
As they haunt the night sky

As Above So Below

The stars seem caught
In strange, obscene orbits
As if crippled by the wishes
Of the madmen of the world

While the moon seems to wear
The face of a mourner
As if the love it conjured
Is now a withered rose

And the sun seems to shine
Like a pale, weakened eye
As if it is a light bulb
On the verge of burning out

For in desperate times
Even nature seems afflicted
As if it too feels helpless
When a shadow grips its heart

Cold Spell

The clouds hang like stained sheets
Over the unmade bed of the world
Where sleepers wander through uneasy dreams
Borrowed from the biographies of the mad

And I wonder when it was the wind began
To speak a language long thought dead
For it seems we are all now puppets again
Guided by an idiot god

But the stars still sparkle like tattooed diamonds
While the flowers turn their faces to the sun
And the laughter of children cascades like water
As pure as their unsullied hearts

For in the great epic of the earth's story
There are both chapters of darkness and dawn
And today's tragedies are tomorrow's reprieves
As they fade like yesterday's news

# Mystery House

His mind was a mansion
Where stairways led to walls
And doors opened to nothing

With rooms full of lights
That would turn on and off
All by themselves

And he wandered its halls
But always returned
Back where he started

As if in a maze
Whose entrance and exit
Were both the same

Secret Identities

There was the one who became a convict
In a prison of his own creation
Who locked the door behind him
And then threw away the key

And the one who became a convert
To a faith with her as its deity
Deciding who was devoted
And who would burn in Hell

And the one who became a subject
In his own scientific experiment
To see if he could find a way
To learn to love the dead

And the one who became a savior
Who longed to wake these children
But found they preferred bondage
To the terror of being free

Diagnosis

There was an animal inside him
That kept changing shape
That wore different faces

A ravenous rat
With a ceaseless hunger
Burrowing through garbage

A cold-blooded snake
Coiled around itself
Drinking its own venom

A maddened dog
Crouched in the shadows
Howling at ghosts

And an earthbound bird
With a broken wing
Dreaming of the sky

Prophecies

In the future people will listen to silence
Watch blank screens on their TV's

Wear clothes the color of their skin
Answer the phone without saying "Hello"

Buy food they throw out without eating
Have children they do not name

Own cars that they never drive
Write letters to random strangers

Go to parties where no one talks
Tour museums of empty frames

Collect items they find on the sidewalk
Read newspapers with the same news each day

Work at jobs without getting paid
Go on vacations without leaving home

Have the identical dream every night
And be buried beneath unmarked tombstones

Time Capsule

She had it all, wireless smart phone,
Electric car with GPS tracking, several
Hundred friends on her Facebook page,
Artificially sweetened energy drinks, thousands
Of MP3 downloads and a high-definition
Flat-screen TV programmed to automatically
Record her favorite reality shows while she slept.

But in her dreams she stood in the heart
Of an abandoned city watching the ghosts
Of old lovers pass by as if they no longer
Knew her, as if they weren't real, strangers
On a road that had no beginning or end,
Like a film she once saw a long time ago
That made her cry but didn't anymore.

Beyond the Sky

I was the one
That saw a young girl
Talking to a tombstone

That heard the slow toll
Of a distant church bell
Beneath the grey clouds

That watched an old woman
Dressed all in black
Buy a bouquet of lilies

That awoke when a siren
Screamed toward the nursing home
But didn't coming back

That read the obituary
Of the reclusive man
That had lived next door to me

That wished I could know
The meaning of the wind
That comes for us all

Narcissist

She sat in her studio
Sketching a self-portrait
Depicting herself as a queen

With a crown full of jewels
And a long red robe
With an ermine collar

She pinned it to the wall
Among hundreds of others
She had drawn over the years

Next to one portraying
Herself as a homeless beggar
On a dark city street

And then she wondered
That if she had to choose
Which one would show the truth

Deciding it would be
The one of a little girl
Trapped with herself in a mirror

Heart of the Night

I hear the cry of a distant train
And think of how life rides a one-way track

Carrying us through a brief landscape
We are given to rent but never to own

Where some spirit places us under a spell
So that we may dance as our days permit

And fall into dreams to let us believe
That the highways we travel lead us to no end

But then we descend to a subterranean realm
As we enter a tunnel swallowed in shadow

To emerge in a place and time unforeseen
We know only from rumors graven in sand

Stalemate

I travel a road
Toward an unknown destination
Unmarked by any sign

Guided by stars
That do not follow
A simple astronomy

Leaving me to consult
Maps in languages
I do not understand

And books of answers
That seem to say
Both yes and no

And as I proceed
I pass the remains
Of others who became lost

Who sought the gold
They believed was promised
Finding only an empty box

Asylum

The tides of life
Bring the skeletons of ships
For they are now ruled
By a lunatic moon

Spreading them over
The shores of the world
Whose bone white beaches
Become graveyards of grey

And each one spills
The bodies of sailors
Their dead eyes still fixed
On the treacherous stars

For the heavens seem caught
In their own dark madness
Mirroring the ones
Driving men to their doom

Last Gasp

I see a realm of ghosts
Longing to find out
Who they were in real life

If they were captains of industry
Or only bitter slaves
Held beneath their sway

For the indifferent wind
Has erased their names
From the cold garden of stones

Leaving them to wonder
If they won life's gamble
Or lost in a fool's wager

And now they look back
As the next world beckons
To bestow its amnesia

Where they will be the same
Shadows without faces
Left to haunt each other

Beneath the Slate Grey Sky

Death is not solely
Reserved for the dying
It wears a thousand
Faces in the world

Like the woman I saw
Alone in a cemetery
Kneeling by a grave
On a cold winter day

She seemed to be speaking
Words in a language
That only the one
Lying buried would know

And when she rose up
To walk away slowly
I could see in her eyes
That she was buried too

Elegy in a Realm of Ashes

By the shores of the river
I can still see the steel mills
Like ghosts in the moonlight
Among the shopping malls

And where there once stood
Furnaces forging girders
A man haunts the restaurants
Where hungry families dine

And he looks at me sadly
While wavering and weaving
By the luxury condos
Built to house the rich

And he seems to be trying
To tell me some story
But a wind out of nowhere
Comes and blows it away

Burden of Hope

As the candles melt into the cake
And the wishbone cracks into splinters

And each penny swallowed by the well
Only makes us one cent poorer

The road from cradle to coffin
Stays a journey we must take in the dark

Through a landscape drained of color
Where even the flowers seem grey

As we lift our eyes to the heaven
Hidden behind its webbing of stars

Asking once more for an answer
To the question a thousand words long

And as we find where we're going
Is the same as where we began

We wrap ourselves in our shadows
To wait for a new sun to rise

Cage of Night

She dressed all in black
To match the dark shadow
Currently in fashion

Advertised on the covers
Of check-out line magazines
That chronicled the latest trends

There was one in particular
That depicted celebrities
In the vestments of priests

Who promoted life styles
Derived from a bible
Whose pages were blank

But deep in her heart
Was a secret star
That she kept to herself

For a time to come
When the wind would change
And the sky would open again

Heartland

I hear the cry
Of a lonely train
Betrayed by its own tracks

As it travels through
Insomniac cities
Afraid of their guilt-ridden dreams

It crosses bridges
Over stricken rivers
Abandoned to bleed in the sun

And over mountains
Resembling idols
Carved by a blind man's hand

Finally it reaches
An empty temple
As grey as a corpse's skin

A forgotten relic
That's now home to ghosts
Each one with a ghost of its own

Touched by the Hand of Madness

He felt he was under
A spell that was cast
By a woman whose love
He had spurned

Who vowed she would seek
A merciless vengeance
So cold he would
Long for death

And when he had
His tarot cards read
They pointed to a
Dark future

As he became a recluse
In the cell of his room
To be haunted by
His own ghost

Entity

Sometimes I hear it
From the apartment above
A man softly strumming
For someone who's not there

And sometimes I see it
In the street down below
A young girl in black
With a liquor store bag

And sometimes I feel it
When the hand of the wind
Scatters the blossoms
Of the magnolia next door

But always I know it
As the light fades away
And another day passes
Without learning its name

City That Care Forgot

I remember its streetcars
Clattering on their tracks
I would ride to the French Quarter
With its antique arcades

And I remember its graveyards
The tombs above ground
That were frequently desecrated
For the jewelry of the dead

And I remember its Mardi Gras
Where costumed masked men
Stood drunkenly on floats
Throwing trinkets to the crowds

And when I had to leave there
A part of me remained
Still sitting on the levee
Caught in the river's spell

Hereafter

In the heart of the night
I hear her voice
As if she had never died

In a siren's howl
Mouthing the wounds
The world inflicted upon her

In a passing car
Its radio blaring
A ballad both whisper and scream

In the lonesome cry
Of a distant train
Trying to escape from itself

And sometimes in the wind
Shaking the trees
That seems to come from nowhere

And in the tears of rain
In a broken rhythm
Falling from an empty sky

House of the Dead

Each room was home
To a different phantom
Buried in its own burden

The one that labored
To leave its heirs
A fortune of priceless sorrow

The one that drowned
In a lifetime of tears
As deep as any ocean

The one that learned
Too late that love
Is a coin that has two sides

But one escaped
Leaving the others
To forever haunt themselves

As it rose from the grave
To begin to compose
A story with a brighter ending

## About the Author

Richard Schnap is a poet, songwriter and collagist living in Pittsburgh, Pennsylvania. A two-time nominee for the Best of the Net award, his poems have most recently appeared locally, nationally and overseas in a variety of print and online publications. His collages can be seen at richardschnap.com.

31245935R00032

Made in the USA
Middletown, DE
23 April 2016